THE LIFE AND WORKS OF

BOTTICELLI

Edmund Swinglehurst

A Compilation of Works from the
BRIDGEMAN ART LIBRARY

Shooting Star Press Inc
230 Fifth Avenue, New York, New York 10001

Botticelli

© Parragon Book Service Ltd 1994

This edition printed for:
Shooting Star Press, Inc.
230 Fifth Avenue - Suite 1212
New York, NY 10001

ISBN   1 56924 171 6

Printed in Italy

Editor: Alexa Stace
Designer: Robert Mathias

The publishers would like to thank Joanna Hartley at the Bridgeman Art Library for her invaluable help

Botticelli 1445-1510

Botticelli

BOTTICELLI LIVED IN ITALY at a time when a rigid medieval culture was giving way to the individualism of a society governed by princes and bishops and inspired by new humanist ideas. Society, which had been formally structured, was experiencing the birth of an open forum where old ideas were now in the melting-pot. This ferment of thought, stirred by Europe's expanding commerce, was reflected in the art of the period.

A revolution in artistic thought had begun earlier in Italy with artists like Giotto and Masaccio, though it did not develop into a common system such as the Gothic had done. Because of the fragmented political nature of Italy, and indeed of northern Europe, split into rival secular and religious city-states, there were as many artistic styles as there were differences of taste and opinion among patrons. This individualism gave European and particularly Italian art a unique diversity which diminished as the High Renaissance concept took over.

Alessandro di Mariano Filipepi was born in Florence in 1444 or 1445, one of eight children born to a tanner. 'Botticelli' was a nickname, probably given him because his brother Antonio, who brought him up, was himself nicknamed 'Botticello' (little barrel). Apart from a year working for the Pope in Rome in 1481-82, Botticelli spent all his life in Florence, which for most of that time was ruled by the powerful Medici family.

The society into which Botticelli was born supported many painters, for there was work in churches, castles, palaces and private mansions, and the young painter must have known the work of many of them, including Fra Angelico who had decorated the convent of San Marco, Antonio and Piero Pollaiuolo in whose workshop he became an apprentice, Signorelli, who was an expert on anatomy, Cosme Tura and Carlo Crivelli, who painted in a decorative medieval style and the Venetians Giorgione and the Bellini brothers who were introducing a new technique derived from northern Europe, where Van Eyck and Van der Weyden had a different approach to painting than that followed in Italy. Botticelli also knew the work of the monk Filippo Lippi, with whom he worked, perhaps as an apprentice, and whose style appealed so much to him that he carried traces of it in his own work all his life.

It is not surprising that he should have borrowed from all these artists aspects of style and technique which were useful to his own individual imagination. Botticelli's own inclinations were towards the pure linear style which he had learned from Lippi and which stemmed from the Sienese school of painting, and he had only a passing interest in the perspective exercises of such contemporaries as Ucello and Piero dell Francesca.

Perhaps because he embodied the old and new ideas in painting, Botticelli soon became well known, partly because one of his first official commissions had been to paint the figures of the assassins who killed Giuliano de' Medici and wounded his brother Lorenzo while at the cathedral in Florence in 1478. The assassins were painted by Botticelli hanging by the neck, in a building alongside the Palazzo dell Signoria, and their jailed accomplices were painted hanging by their feet.

In 1492 Lorenzo the Magnificent died and Florence found itself facing invasion by Charles VIII of France. Lorenzo's successor, Piero de' Medici, was driven out of Florence. In the midst of the ensuing turmoil there appeared a fanatical monk, Savonarola, who prophesied doom for Florence unless Florentines gave up their sinful life and love of luxury, including art. Though initially gathering a large following, which according to Vasari, the Renaissance chronicler, included Botticelli, Savonarola was eventually hanged and burned in 1498 by order, it was said, of the Pope himself. After this extraordinary episode there is a considerable lack of knowledge about Botticelli's life. His popularity as a painter began to decline, though whether this had anything to do with the Savonarola drama or with changing fashions which were favouring new painters like Titian, Michelangelo and Raphael, is not known.

Alessandro Botticelli died in May 1510 and, as an artist, virtually disappeared from view for 300 years. Interest in him revived only in the mid-19th century, when he was rediscovered by the Pre-Raphaelite painters Millais and Rossetti and reinstated as one of the more rare talents of the 15th century in Italy.

NOTE: Most of Botticelli's work which is described as 'panel' in the captions was done on poplar panels. These were primed with gesso on which the drawing was incised with a sharp instrument. A monochrome underlay was added, and then the tempera colour, which was thinned with egg yolk and oil.

◁ **Adoration of the Magi**
c 1465

Panel

THIS IS PROBABLY the first of Botticelli's five versions of the subject. It is also the widest, as it is painted on a narrow rectangular panel, the dimensions no doubt dictated by the space it was intended to fill. Botticelli has divided his picture into three sections. On the left, the three kings' retinue arrives in a great crowd of people and horses flowing down to the front of the picture. The centre section shows the kings, having passed by a broken wall, in the presence of the seated Mother and Child, set on the right of centre. Behind her, in the third section, Botticelli has left the space surprisingly empty, perhaps to emphasize the isolation of the Madonna and Child and the dark ominous blackness of the cave behind the stable entrance.

◁ **Fortitude** 1470

Panel

THIS IS THE EARLIEST documented work by Sandro Botticelli. It was his contribution to a series of allegorical figures of the virtues, commissioned by the powerful guild, the Arte della Mercanzia. There were seven figures, two commissioned from Botticelli and five from Piero Pollaiuolo, one of two brothers who ran one of the most advanced artistic workshops of the day in Florence. But the original commission for all seven had been with Piero Pollaiuolo, who protested at two of them being given to Botticelli, and the latter eventually did only *Fortitude*. It is a much superior work to Piero's six, as visitors to the Uffizi Gallery in Florence may see for themselves, since all seven pictures hang together in the gallery. Even the fact that Botticelli evidently took great care to paint in the manner appropriate to a product of the Pollaiuolo studio cannot disguise his much greater ability as an artist.

▷ **Judith with the Head of Holofernes** c 1470-2

Panel

JUDITH WAS A BIBLICAL heroine who, when her town of Bethulia was being attacked by Holofernes, a general of Nebuchadnezzar's army, stole into the enemy camp and cut off his head while he slept. Botticelli's painting gives us a battle scene outside the walls of the besieged town as a lively background. Judith, with an olive branch representing peace in one hand, and a sword in the other, is leading her maid, who is carrying Holofernes's head, away from the action, in which the people of Bethulia, inspired by Judith's heroism, are slaughtering the invaders. The style of the painting has more of the energy of Piero Pollaiuolo than the quiet tenderness of Filippo Lippi, an indication that Botticelli was clever at adapting to whatever style he considered appropriate to the painting he was engaged on.

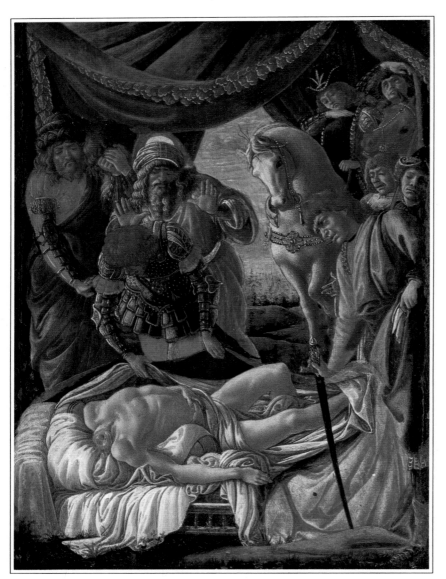

◁ The Discovery of the Body of Holofernes c 1470-2

Panel

THIS COMPANION PICTURE to *Judith with the Head of Holofernes* shows the influence of the Pollaiuolo brothers, in whose studio Botticelli had learned his art. The expressions on the faces of Holofernes's generals are the work of a young Botticelli who has not yet acquired the cool dispassionate view of tragic events that was evident in his later work. The ornate costumes are also something that Botticelli was to discard later, when he dressed his characters in simpler clothes. The figure leaning forward over the body shows that the artist had at least a passing interest in the challenges of perspective in presenting foreshortened figures as Mantegna had done in his painting of the dead Christ.

▷ **Madonna del Mare** 1470

Panel

THIS *Madonna of the Sea* seems to be an early Botticelli, for there is a certain stiffness in the pose, and the folds of the clothing lack the flowing gracefulness that characterized his later paintings. The Christ child, who is dropping seeds from his right hand, which he has taken from the whole fruit held in his left, has the elongated body which Botticelli later adopted in his more mannered style. The background scene shows an unknown coastline with curious gothic-style buildings and a ship, suggesting that it might have been painted for a guild connected with maritime affairs.

▷ **Madonna and Child with Saint Mary Magdalen, Saint John the Baptist, Saint Cosmas, Saint Damian, Saint Francis of Assisi, and Saint Catherine of Alexandria** c 1470-2

Tempera on panel

THIS IS BOTTICELLI'S first surviving altarpiece. Though it is sometimes known as the *Altarpiece of the Convertiti* (an order of nuns named after Elizabeth the Converted), there is no sure identification. The Madonna is larger than the surrounding saints and with the two red-cloaked saints, Cosmas and Damian, at her feet forms the apex of a triangle which dominates the composition. Saint Mary Magdalen is on the left of the picture holding a censer, and Saint Catherine of Alexandria has her hand on the spiked wheel on which she was tortured when she refused to give up her faith and marry the Emperor Maxentius. Cosmas and Damian were patron saints of the Medici, so that the saints' faces here may be Medici portraits, but as the two saints were patron saints of physicians also, there may be no Medici connection after all.

◁ **Madonna of the Eucharist**
c 1472

Panel

THE TITLE OF THIS PAINTING is
symbolized by the wheat and
grapes which the Madonna is
touching so delicately, for they
are the natural sources of
bread and wine, the two most
important elements of the
Eucharist. The composition of
the painting is interesting: the
figures have been brought
forward, as if they were
portrait studies, and into close
contact with the viewer. The
Madonna and Child, though
rather separated in the
composition, are brought
together by the architectural
feature in the background.
Beyond this Botticelli has
created a sense of space by
painting a landscape which is
an integral part of the painting
and not just a background.

▷ **Portrait of a Man Holding a Medal** c 1473-4

Tempera on panel

THIS IS A MOST unusual portrait, because its dominant feature is the medal, which carries a portrait of Cosimo de' Medici, founder of the family that ruled Florence during its most brilliant artistic period. Although there are few records of Botticelli's dealing with the Medici, there is no doubt that as one of Florence's leading painters he benefitted from their patronage. He painted the heads of Cosimo and other members of the Medici family into an *Adoration of the Magi* commissioned by Guaspare di Zanobi del Lama, a friend of the Medici. This easel portrait - unusual in itself in that portrait painting was still very much part of the narrative fresco tradition – is not Cosimo de' Medici himself, however. The sitter has not been identified. The medal is a gilt gesso cast of a medal of Cosimo de' Medici made about 1465. When the panel for the painting was prepared, a raised circle of wood was left on it for the medal cast to be applied to.

▷ **Portrait of Giuliano de' Medici** c 1475

Panel

ART HISTORIANS have come to doubt that this is, in fact, a portrait of Giuliano, who was assassinated by the Pazzi conspirators during their attack on the brothers while at prayer in the cathedral in 1478. The profile does not resemble the Giuliano portrayed in the del Lama-commissioned *Adoration of the Magi*, nor the one on the medal commemorating his death. Nevertheless, popular opinion has always thought of this as a portrait of Giuliano; there have even been other copies made of it, probably in the 19th century, claiming to be Giuliano portraits. Giuliano was supposed to be in love with Simonetta Vespucci, the wife of a friend of the Medicis, but this could have been an idealized love, impossible to satisfy, as with Dante and Beatrice or Petrarch and Laura.

◁ **Portrait of a Young Woman**
c 1476-8

Panel

THIS AUSTERE, brown-toned portrait of a young woman is sometimes said to be of Simonetta Vespucci, much admired by Giuliano de' Medici. She looks a much more severe person than the woman in Botticelli's other supposed portrait of Simonetta (see page 42) and not, one feels, a likely protagonist in the grand passion described by Poliziano in his poem 'La Giostra', which commemorates a lavish tourney Giuliano organized in her honour. It is likely that neither of the young women portrayed was in fact Simonetta: she was so genuinely lovely that years after her death, Botticelli chose to commemorate her beauty by using her as a model for the *Primavera*. Vasari added to the Simonetta controversy by referring to two paintings kept by Cosimo de' Medici in his wardrobe, one of which, said Vasari, was Simonetta and the other Lorenzo de' Medici's wife.

◁ **Adoration of the Magi**
1476-7

Panel

THIS *Adoration of the Magi* was commissioned by Guaspare di Zanobi del Lama for an altar in the church of Santa Maria Novella in Florence. He was a friend of the Medici family, which may explain why the three kings have the features of three distinguished members of the Medici family. Cosimo, the elder and founder of the Medici dynasty, is paying homage to the Christ child; in the foreground are Giuliano, who was assassinated in the Pazzi conspiracy, and Giovanni, son of Cosimo. Vasari first suggested the portrait identification in his *Lives of the Artists*, some 70 years after the picture was painted. He also suggested that the man standing on the extreme right of the picture was the artist himself. Although Vasari, the main near-contemporary source of information about painters of the Renaissance, is not always considered absolutely reliable, there is no doubt that the profile of Cosimo is the same as that appearing in *Portrait of a Man Holding a Medal* (page 17).

▷ **Portrait of Dante** c 1480-5

Oil on canvas

LIKE SOME OTHER Botticelli portraits, it is uncertain whether this was actually painted by him. The attribution has come as a result of the artist's known admiration for the great poet and because of his superb illustrations for Dante's *The Divine Comedy*, principally the Cantos entitled 'Paradise' and 'Inferno'. Artist and poet may also have shared some radical political ideas. Dante, a great champion of Florentine independence, had spent much of his life in exile after the inter-family struggles which had bedevilled much of Florentine life in the late 13th century resulted in one group gaining control at the expense of the group Dante had supported. The painting could have been done from other paintings and medallions by Botticelli's studio. The matter is further confused by the fact that several other copies of Dante's portrait exist, some of them known to have been painted in the 19th century at the time of Botticelli's 'rediscovery'.

◁ **Dante and Beatrice, from Dante's *Divine Comedy*** 1480

Drawing in pen and ink

BOTTICELLI'S DRAWINGS for Dante's *Divine Comedy* were probably made for Lorenzo di Pierfrancesco de' Medici, who had also commissioned the *Primavera* and *Birth of Venus*. Botticelli's work was neglected for over 300 years after his death, and the drawings had been lost sight of until they turned up at a sale of a Scottish collection to the Berlin Museum in 1884. The drawings, which show off Botticelli's genius for line drawing so magnificently, were intended for a de luxe volume which was never completed. The Botticelli treatment of the illustrations was innovative at the time: he gave each one a page to itself and did not intermix drawings and text, as was then the custom. In this drawing, Beatrice, object of Dante's ideal but unconsummated love, takes the poet on a trip round Paradise escorted by angels.

▷ **Primavera** c 1480

Tempera on wood on a gesso ground

THE *Primavera* WAS probably commissioned by Lorenzo di Pierfrancesco de' Medici, whose father was the son of Cosimo de' Medici's illegitimate brother and therefore Lorenzo the Magnificent's second cousin. He was Botticelli's greatest private patron; without him Botticelli might never have painted the *Primavera* and other secular works that are regarded as his masterpieces. As a painting of considerable size (204 x 314 cm/70 x 123 in) the *Primavera* was unusual for a secular painting and also striking in its subject matter. The main theme, though others have been put forward by art historians, is love and marriage and the painting is dominated at its centre by the figure of Venus and her son Cupid. Botticelli evidently based the whole on ideas from Greek mythology and created a work which while suggestively erotic in some aspects also presents the theme in a way that would not have upset Florentine susceptibilities.

◁ **Primavera** (detail):
The Three Graces c 1478-80

Tempera on wood

THE THREE GRACES,
represented by nubile young
women in loose white
garments symbolic of virginity,
are the targets for Cupid's
dart. As acolytes of Venus, the
Graces embody the sexual
powers of springtime and at
the same time the virtues
inherent in their personae.
Though similar in appearance,
because Botticelli modelled
most of his female figures on
the beautiful Simonetta
Vespucci who had died at the
age of 24, the Graces are three
individual characters whom
Seneca, the Roman writer,
referred to as Aglaia,
Euphrosyne and Thalia.
Mercury, standing by them but
facing outwards, is their
protector and also the
guardian of the garden in
which spring is arriving. His
presence could also be
explained by the legend that
he had fathered Venus's son
Cupid.

▷ **Primavera** (detail): **Zephyr, Chloris and Flora** c 1480

Tempera on wood

THE FIGURES ON THE RIGHT-HAND side of the *Primavera* represent a transformation scene. Zephyr, the breeze of spring, is approaching the nymph Chloris who, fearing his intentions, tries to cry out, but only roses spill out of her mouth. Having lost her virginity she becomes Flora, goddess of spring, who, now fully dressed in glorious apparel and wearing the jewellery of a married woman of Florentine society, is a symbol of motherhood and, by her distribution of the roses gathered in her skirt, the good things of life. Thus, though the painting was done for the privacy of a Medici house it is not a show of *dolce vita* but a charming account of the process of love and marriage.

Detail

▷ **Athena and the Centaur** 1482

Canvas

THIS BEAUTIFUL COMPANION piece to the secular paintings *Primavera* and *Birth of Venus* was also painted for Lorenzo di Pierfrancesco de' Medici. Pallas Athena, daughter of Zeus, goddess of wisdom and protector of the arts, is seen here with a centaur, a creature half man and half beast. In Botticelli's painting, Pallas is evidently passing on to the centaur, by touch, the knowledge which makes men human but also creates in them a conscience and sense of morality. The awareness of this new attribute is evidently causing the centaur some inner conflict - a condition with which Botticelli, a Neoplatonist and humanist, would have been familiar.

◁ **The Madonna of the Magnificat** c 1482

Panel

THIS SKILFULLY COMPOSED tondo is perhaps the most successful of Botticelli's Madonna paintings. The tender lines of the Madonna's arms curving round the infant Christ lead on to the hand of one of the handsome angels and through his own and his companion's arms to the Madonna's crown, creating a surging circular movement, a kind of whirlpool around the calm vortex of the landscape in the distance. As in the *Madonna of the Pomegranate* (see page 50), the Christ child holds the fruit in his hand as a symbol of the immortality that he will bring to mankind.

▷ **Madonna of the Magnificat**
(detail) 1482

THE HEAD OF the *Madonna of the Magnificat* embodies all the qualities that Botticelli looked for in women. There is the smooth, pale skin and firm but delicate structure of the face. The expression is pure and virginal but in the rounded lips there is a hint of sensuousness. The thick coils of hair have an earthy touch, as if they belong to a peasant girl, while the scarf and delicate veil, like fashion accessories, seem to transform the flesh and blood woman whom Botticelli has taken for his Madonna into an idealized one.

◁ **Madonna del Libro** 1482

Tempera on panel

THIS PAINTING'S usual English title is *Virgin Teaching the Child to Read*. In an age when the majority of the population was illiterate, to be able to read was an accomplishment which most people regarded with respect not unmixed with awe. The written word was in the custody of the Church and learned men and was a symbol of power and authority. Botticelli intends the book in this painting, which has been identified as a book of hours called 'the Hours of the Virgin', to symbolize the authority of the Church's knowledge derived from the Bible and other holy books. The cherries behind the book are also a symbol (the promise of Paradise which Christ brings) and the nails in the child's hand and crown of thorns round his wrist represent the suffering by which the sins of the earth will be redeemed and Paradise regained.

▷ **Portrait of a Young Man**
1482

Panel

ABOUT THE TIME that Botticelli was painting the frescoes in the Sistine Chapel in Rome, he also painted a number of portraits of young men, like this youth in a red hat. None of the sitters has been identified; perhaps they were colleagues working with him in his studio or friends met in Rome. They all have the air of being drawn from life and their frank, direct gaze suggests that they were on familiar terms with the painter. Unlike portraits intended to represent the subject's status in life or to project a particular character, these impress the onlooker as being portraits of people posing unselfconsciously and with no thought of how the painter is portraying them.

▷ **Nastagio degli Onesti,
First Episodes** c 1483

Tempera on panel

THE *Nastagio degli Onesti* panels
were painted for the spalliera
(wainscotting) of the marriage
chamber of Giannozo Pucci
and his bride, Lucrezia de
Piero Bini. Their subject, a tale
from Boccaccio's *Decameron*,
hardly seems appropriate to
the occasion but perhaps it was
in keeping with the doctrine of
female obedience prevalent at
the time. There are four
panels, presumably one for
each wall of the chamber, three
of which are in the Prado
Museum in Madrid.

This first panel illustrates
the first scenes of the story. A
despondent young man
walking alone in the woods is
surprised to see a knight on
horseback, accompanied by his
hounds, chasing a young
woman through the forest. It
appears that the young woman
is trying to escape the knight
who wants to marry her,
though she has scorned him.
She is brought down by the
hounds.

◁ **Nastagio degli Onesti, Further Episodes** c 1483

Tempera on panel

IN THIS SECOND PANEL of the *Nastagio degli Onesti* series the young woman has her heart removed by the knight as a punishment for rejecting his proposal. The dogs, on the right of the panel, are fed her entrails and in the background is a flashback to the beginning of the chase. Her dismemberment and disembowelling is to be the young woman's punishment for scorning the knight, and will be repeated in the third panel of the series.

▷ **Nastagio degli Onesti,
Further Episodes II** 1483

Tempera on panel

THE YOUNG MAN, who is also
pining for his beloved, decides
to hold a banquet in the forest
next time the knight chases his
reluctant young woman, his
object being to allow his own
beloved and her family and
friends to witness the moral
tale. The banquet is held, the
loved one takes it to heart and
decides that she will marry her
young man. All ends happily,
as is shown in the last panel of
the series, which depicts a
sumptuous banquet held in
honour of the newly married
company.

◁ **Nastagio degli Onesti,
The Wedding Feast** c 1483

Panel

IN THE FINAL scene of the
Nastagio degli Onesti series,
Botticelli has used an
architectural setting similar to
the one which appears in one
of his Nativity paintings. The
architecture is not so much a
building as simply a decorative
device to contain the action.
The diners, at two long tables,
are attending the wedding
banquet of the gloomy young
man (in the first painting of
the series) and his young
bride, who has been
persuaded into accepting him
by the terrible story. The
young servants bringing on
the dishes for the wedding
feast look like the youths who
appear as Botticelli angels in
other paintings and the blue
skies seen through the
colonnades add to the happy
implications of the scene.

▷ **Portrait of a Young Woman**
1485

Tempera on panel

THIS DISHEVELLED young
woman is the other candidate
for being a portrait of
Simonetta Vespucci, who
inspired such a strong
admiration in Giuliano de'
Medici (see page 18). With her
wild and fiery looks, she seems
a more romantic choice for the
role of the beloved of Lorenzo
the Magnificent's brother
Giuliano than does the rather
plain subject of *Portrait of a
Young Woman*. Giuliano's
assassination in the cathedral
in Florence in 1478 added to
the lustre of the story of
romantic lovers and created a
band of loyal supporters for
this portrait as a depiction of
the true Simonetta. In fact
there is little firm evidence to
suggest that either portrait is
the real Simonetta. Indeed,
according to Vasari, if one of
them was, nobody would have
known it, for Botticelli never
revealed the names of his
sitters. It is possible, too, that it
was worked on by painters
other than Botticelli, for it is
usually assigned to the
Botticelli workshop rather
than to the artist himself.

▷ **The Virgin and Child Surrounded by Five Angels**
date unknown

THIS IS NOT a typically idealized 'Madonna and Child' picture. The rather sleepy child holding the pomegranate and the tired and irritated-looking mother are a real life observation by Botticelli, who lived at home and no doubt knew all about the stresses and strains of domestic life. Even the angels at the back look like choirboys at the end of a long and tedious practice. The composition of the picture is reminiscent of Sienese paintings, in which the main character occupies most of the picture space and others are fitted in behind like a two-dimensional background with no attempt to create an all-enveloping atmosphere.

△ **Birth of Venus** c 1484-6

Tempera on canvas

THIS IS PROBABLY the most famous of all Botticelli's paintings, though it represents only one small stratum of his work. The *Venus* is a secular painting done for Lorenzo di Pierfrancesco de' Medici, like the *Primavera* (page 24). The painting was commissioned for the private delectation of the patron, and was therefore not seen except by his friends and the servants of his household. Botticelli's religious paintings followed precise rules and each carried a message, but the *Birth of Venus* was painted for pleasure, though within the philosophy of human freedom popular with the Neoplatonists who interpreted the birth of Venus as Humanitas - a union of spiritual and sensual qualities.

▷ **Birth of Venus** (detail)
c 1484-6

Tempera on canvas

THE FIGURE THAT APPEARS on
the right of the *Birth of Venus*,
about to cover the nakedness
of the goddess with a flowered
cloak, is one of the three
Horae nymphs of the seasons
and like the Graces, attendants
to Venus. This one, judging by
her dress which is decorated
with spring flowers, is the
nymph of the season when the
powers that Venus controls are
at their most potent. The
presence of the Hora of spring
does not mean, however, that
Venus was born in this season;
it merely refers to the Homeric
poem from which Botticelli
perhaps derived his
inspiration and which refers to
Zephyr wafting Venus to the
land of Cyprus where she is
received by the Horae.
Botticelli evidently decided
that one Hora was enough for
his composition.

◁ **Mars and Venus** c 1485-6

Panel

PAINTED AT ABOUT the same time as the *Primavera*, this painting has the same characteristics and feeling of intimacy as other secular paintings by Botticelli. Though apparently pagan, these paintings were conceived within the framework of the Neoplatonist philosophy of the time, which was acceptable within the Christian doctrine of the Church. Cosimo de' Medici, who approved of the new thinking, appointed Masilio Ficino to instruct young Florentines of good family in the new philosophy. Thus Botticelli's paintings were socially acceptable. In this painting, Botticelli presents the idea of war and peace in Mars and Venus. He, exhausted by the stress of warfare and oblivious even to the rowdy bambini has given in, while she, alert and dynamic, represents the positive aspects of a peaceful life.

▷ The Extraction of the Heart of Saint Ignatius c 1487

Panel

THE LONG WOODEN panels that filled in space at the bottom of altarpieces often left the artist with a problem. Mostly these were filled with busy scenes of the particular saint's life, but Botticelli preferred to keep them simple, focusing on one action. In this case, the action is the removal of the heart of Saint Ignatius, probably Saint Ignatius of Antioch, an elderly man who ended his days as a martyr in Rome where he was thrown to the lions. The panel was done, like *The Vision of Saint Augustine*, for the altarpiece of the Church of San Barnaba.

◁ **The Madonna of the Pomegranate** 1487

Panel

Detail

THIS TONDO, though not as successful a composition as the *Madonna of the Magnificat*, nevertheless has great charm, despite the Virgin's apparent detachment from the scene around her. The lively faces of the young men with their books are well observed and look like portraits, possibly belonging to the same group of young men as those in individual portraits painted by Botticelli at about this time. There is no record of whether this painting was a public or private commission, though the lilies carved in its original frame, in which it still hangs, suggest it may have hung in the audience hall of the Palazzo Vecchio, the fortified headquarters of the government of Florence.

▷ **The Vision of Saint Augustine** 1488

Panel

THIS PAINTED PANEL is one of four surviving from the predella of the San Barnaba Church Altarpiece. Saint Augustine is seen here on a deserted shore where he has been walking and meditating on the mystery of the Holy Trinity and how as a doctor of the Church he can explain it to his flock. Coming across a child digging a hole, he asks what it is for. The child replies that he intends to put the ocean in it, at which Saint Augustine smiles and tells him that this is impossible. No more impossible, the child answers, than the problem that the saint is trying to resolve; then the child vanishes. To people in Botticelli's time such stories and ideas were given exposure by the work of artists who were, in a sense, popularizers of ideas.

Detail

▷ **Madonna and Child with Angels and Saint John the Baptist** 1488-90

Panel

THIS UNUSUAL TONDO shows the Madonna with the Child holding a pomegranate and a young Saint John the Baptist. In the background, a group of angels sit on benches, looking like a group of schoolboys. The books add to the impression of intellectual pursuit and emphasize Botticelli's personal interest in learning, especially the new learning of Neoplatonic humanism, an interest which some historians also identify with the secular paintings that Botticelli did for Lorenzo di Pierfrancesco de' Medici. It is probable that this painting was a product of Botticelli's workshop, with the master perhaps sketching in the ground composition and leaving his apprentices to do much of the painting.

◁ **The Annunciation
(Cestello Annunciation)**
1489-90

Tempera on panel

Detail

THE SWIRLING movement within the painting of Gabriel, the Virgin and their clothing is typically Botticelli: the brilliant accomplishment of a polished and meticulous technique. This is perhaps the most intensely felt of Botticelli's several versions of the subject. It was commissioned in 1489 as an altarpiece for a chapel in a Cistercian church, the Cestello in Florence (now called Santa Maria Maddalena dei Pazzi). The man who commissioned the work, Benedotto di Sar Francesco Guardi, paid Botticelli 30 ducats for his work, only 20 ducats less than the Guardi had paid for his chapel (with a stained-glass window) in the Cestello. At a time when other Florentine painters were moving towards the more realistic approach of Venetians like Giorgione and the Bellinis, Botticelli seems here to be more dedicated than ever to a linear style derived from the Sienese and North European painters. This may account for his eclipse in the art world from the 16th century to the 19th, most art lovers having been won over to the realism of Titian, Tintoretto and their followers.

◁ **Saint Jerome in Penitence**
c 1490-3

Tempera on panel

THIS IS ANOTHER predella panel of the San Marco Altarpiece. Saint Jerome was a highly intellectual priest who translated practically all the Bible from Hebrew and Greek into Latin. A contradictory man, he cared for the poor and ignorant, but was also irascible and argumentative and after violent discussions would feel guilty at his pride. In repentance, he would beat himself on the chest with a stone, a punishment which Botticelli portrays in this painting. When Pope Sixtus V saw Botticelli's work he commented that Jerome had done well to use the stone, otherwise he would never have been numbered among the saints. Unusually among his panel paintings, Botticelli has painted a whole scene here, with an architectural setting and views of a distant city, perhaps Rome, where Jerome was secretary to the Pope.

▷ **Coronation of the Virgin**
c 1490-3

Tempera on panel

THIS OPULENT WORK is the main picture of the San Marco Altarpiece which the guild of goldsmiths commissioned Botticelli to paint for the chapel of Saint Eligius, their patron saint, in the prestigious convent of San Marco (see page 66). The *Coronation* is deliberately divided into two sections, one representing the heavenly realm and the other the earthly one where the representatives of God guide the people. The Church fathers are imposing presences. From the left: Saint John the Evangelist is shown with suitably impassioned gestures; Saint Augustine writes in a book, thus showing his scholarly work; Saint Jerome gazes in wonder heavenwards; and Saint Eligius, patron of the goldsmiths, looks out of the picture towards worshippers in the chapel, his hand raised in blessing. Above, God the Father, wearing a papal-like crown, blessing the Virgin while placing a superb gold crown set with pearls on her head.

◁ **Saint Augustine Writing in His Cell** c 1490-3

Tempera on panel

SAINT AUGUSTINE in this small painting seems a very much more humble person than the one that Botticelli had painted in 1480 as a powerful leader and doctor of the Church. Saint Augustine, not to be confused with Saint Augustine of Canterbury, was a highly intellectual Church leader of the 4th century AD. He was a prolific writer of works on religion; over 100 books and 200 letters of his are in existence. Botticelli, who was an admirer of his work, has shown him here as a writer going through the usual stresses of composition, discarding what is unsatisfactory in screwed-up pieces of paper on the floor.

▷ St John the Theologian on Patmos Writing the Book of Revelations c 1490-3

Panel

THIS LONG PANEL, a predella panel from the San Marco Altarpiece, shows Saint John, also called the Divine, in solitude on the island of Patmos. The sea surrounds the green island and he sits alone amid austere and barren rocks: an appropriate setting for the author of the apocalyptic book which follows what is called the fourth gospel. Saint John, who was a scholar started off his discipleship when he and his brother James left their fishing business in order to follow Jesus Christ. It has been suggested that the simple style of these predella paintings may have been a response to the more complex work of the young Leonardo da Vinci.

Detail

▷ **Madonna del Padiglione** c 1493

Tempera on panel

THE RED CANOPY spreading out above and behind the Madonna looks like a medieval tent, making an arresting shape within the circle of this tondo (also called Virgin and Child with Three Angels). The canopy does not close off the painting, as a wall hanging might have done; by allowing a glimpse of the countryside beyond, it gives a sense of space which adds to the open-air feeling of the painting. The angels to each side make an active contrast to the domestic scene in the centre where the Madonna is preparing to breastfeed an impatient child in the care of an angel. The book in the background, symbolizing learning, is perhaps a reference to the child's progress through life from babyhood to youth.

▷ The Miracle of Saint Eligius c 1493

Tempera on panel

THIS IS ONE of the five predella panels Botticelli made for the altarpiece of a chapel in the convent of San Marco in Florence. In lively style it shows the saint, who was Bishop of Limoges, mending a horse's foreleg. Apart from his religious work, Saint Eligius was renowned for his skill as a blacksmith and metal-worker, talents which brought him the admiration and friendship of King Dagobert of the Franks who protected and promoted him in his kingdom. Eligius's skills also made him a patron saint of metal-workers and engravers, which explains his presence here. The altarpiece was commissioned by the guild of goldsmiths for the recently rebuilt chapel of their patron saint in San Marco.

◁ **Pietà: Lamentation over the Dead Christ** c 1495

Panel

THERE ARE TWO Botticelli *Pietàs*, each one a superb example of the artist's later work and showing a talent for composing close groups of figures. This *Pietà* was painted for an altar in the church of Santa Maria Maggiore, where it was seen and commented on by Vasari. It is an unusually emotional picture for Botticelli, whose cool, calm virgins are almost his trademark. All the figures in the painting, including Saint Joseph of Arimathea holding the crown of thorns and the nails from the Cross, are expressing deeply felt emotion.

Detail

▷ The Calumny of Apelles
c 1494-5

Panel

ACCORDING TO VASARI, this painting was given by Botticelli to a friend called Antonio Segni. It is the last of his secular paintings to have survived. The subject was taken from a lost work by the Greek artist Apelles, known because of a description of it by the Roman Lucian. It was this description which gave Botticelli the theme for the work. According to the story, the painter Apelles was accused by a rival painter of disloyalty to his patron, Ptolemy IV, Philopator of Egypt. To refute the charge, he made a painting, entitled 'Calumny'. In Botticelli's version of the story, the victim is seen being dragged across the floor by Calumny, who is carrying a torch, while Ptolemy is listening to malicious gossips. The figure of Truth, looking like Venus, is standing apart with an old, grief-stricken woman, Remorse, in front of her.

The Tragedy of Lucretia
c 1496

Tempera on panel

▷ *Overleaf, see pages 72-3*

THIS PANEL, according to Vasari, was one of several commissioned by Guidantonio Vespucci to decorate one of the rooms in his house. The story deals with the theme of dishonour. Lucretia, wife of Brutus, has been dishonoured by being raped by Tarquin Superbus (the figure in yellow tunic and red cloak on the left) and commits suicide. Infuriated by the tragedy, Junius Brutus drives the Tarquins out of Rome. This ancient Roman legend inspired many artists, including Titian and Tintoretto, who used a theme so relevant to the Italian attitude to their womenfolk in numerous works. In this painting, Botticelli shows a great interest in the architectural setting, creating a Roman city street scene in which the body of Lucretia is the central point of the action, but is overshadowed by the splendid buildings on all sides.

▷ **Mystical Nativity** c 1501

Tempera on canvas

DESPITE THE DECLINING success of his later years, or perhaps because of his increasing religious faith, Botticelli's later paintings have an optimistic note. In this wonderful *Nativity*, Botticelli emphasizes the theme of man's relationship with God. The angels are in festive mood, and carry olive branches, symbols of peace. In the foreground, three humans embrace three angels in a reconciliation between man burdened with original sin and the angels who represent redemption and the eternal life. The angels carry scrolls with the angels' words to the shepherds from St Luke's Gospel: 'On earth peace to men of goodwill.' The defeated evils writhe on the ground near them, except for one who seems to have hopes of another opportunity to promote sin.

◁ **Mystical Nativity** (detail)
c 1501

Tempera on canvas

THIS DETAIL from inside the stable, depicting the Virgin and Child, with Joseph apparently asleep on the left, shows how Botticelli ignored all the newly discovered rules of perspective, achieving the effect of recession and depth by other means. He leads the spectator's eye into the picture by means of the path which zig-zags into the cave in front of which the stable is built. The trees in the background, seen through the cave, give a sense of distance and extra depth to the composition. As with Sienese artists, Botticelli has also ignored the relative size of the figures in the picture; the Virgin is much larger than Joseph, as an indication of her importance. Though ignoring the rules, Botticelli has created a fine original work of art.

◁ **Transfiguration** c 1500

Tempera on panel

CHRIST APPEARING with Elisha in his goatskin and Moses may not be strictly according to the Biblical account, but Botticelli has made this the scene for this small triptych (27 cm/ 10 ½ in high), which also includes three disciples, James, Peter and John, disposed in the manner of the disciples in the *Agony in the Garden* (see page 78). The flanking panels (the shutters) show Saint Jerome and Saint Augustine, the two great scholars of the Church, old and venerable figures compared to the young risen Christ. Though separated from the main panel, the figures form part of the composition of the whole, their heads forming part of a triangle of which Christ's head is the apex.

◁ **Agony in the Garden** c 1504

Panel

THIS UNUSUAL PAINTING decorated the chapel which houses the bodies of Ferdinand and Isabella, the Spanish Catholic monarchs who are credited with driving the Moors out of Granada and uniting Spain. The chapel, which stands by the cathedral in Granada, was built at Isabella's orders in 1504, during Botticelli's lifetime. The setting of the *Agony in the Garden*, with the Mount of Olives depicted as a rocky mound surrounded by wooden palings, has a sculptural quality reminiscent of the work of Mantegna, who died in 1306; the meticulous detail of the flora and the landscape characterizes the harder line of Botticelli's late paintings.